Contents

What is rock?

Rock is a material.

Exploring Materials

Rock

Abby Colich

Raintree is an imprint of Capstone Global Library Limited, a company incorporated in England and Wales having its registered office at 7 Pilgrim Street, London, EC4V 6LB Registered company number: 6695582

www.raintreepublishers.co.uk
myorders@raintreepublishers.co.uk

Text © Capstone Global Library Limited 2014
First published in hardback in 2014
Paperback edition first published in 2015
The moral rights of the proprietor have been asserted.

Edited by Abby Colich, Dan Nunn, and Catherine Veitch
Designed by Marcus Bell
Picture research by Tracy Cummins
Production by Victoria Fitzgerald
Originated by Capstone Global Library Ltd
Printed and bound in China

ISBN 978 1 4062 6335 0 (hardback)
17 16 15 14 13
10 9 8 7 6 5 4 3 2 1

ISBN 978 1 4062 6343 5 (paperback)
18 17 16 15 14
10 9 8 7 6 5 4 3 2 1

British Library Cataloguing in Publication Data
Colich, Abby.
Rock. – (Exploring materials)
552-dc23
A full catalogue record for this book is available from the British Library.

Acknowledgements
We would like to thank the following for permission to reproduce photographs: Shutterstock pp. 4 (© orxy), 5 (© ross-edward cairney), 6 (© ermess), 7a (© Ho Yeow Hui), 7b (© Bejim), 7c (© Natalia Bratslavsky), 7d (© Brian K.), 8 (© Matyas Arvai), 9 (© Dumitrescu Ciprian-Florin), 10 (© Goluba), 11 (© IMAGENFX), 12 (© Golden Pixels LLC), 13 (© Juha-Pekka Kervinen), 14 (© RUI FERREIRA), 15 (© Andreja Donko), 16 (© Patryk Kosmider), 17 (© feiyuwzhangjie), 18 (© Marie C Fields), 19r (© Ruslan Kudrin), 19l (© Chianuri), 20 (Ariy), 21 (© Coffeemill), 22 (© Ivica Drusany, © Evgeniya Uvarova, © Shaun Dodds), 23a (© Andreja Donko), 23b (© Marie C Fields).

Front cover photograph of a boy stacking a pile of stones reproduced with permission of Getty Images (© Geoff Brighting).

Back cover photograph reproduced with permission of Shutterstock (© Marie C Fields).

We would like to thank Valarie Akerson, Nancy Harris, Dee Reid, and Diana Bentley for their assistance in the preparation of this book.

Every effort has been made to contact copyright holders of material reproduced in this book. Any omissions will be rectified in subsequent printings if notice is given to the publisher.

Materials are what things are
made from.

There are many different kinds
of rock.

Rock can be made into many different things.

Where does rock come from?

Rock is found in nature.

Rock is found underground.

Rock is found underwater.

People dig rock out of the ground.

What is rock like?

chalk

Rock can be soft or hard.

Chalk is soft rock.

smooth

Rock can be smooth or rough.

Rock can break into smaller pieces.

Rock can be carved into different shapes.

How do we use rock?

We use rock to build houses.

We use rock to build bridges.

Chalk comes from rock.

rock salt

table salt

Some salt comes from rock.

We use rock to make art.

We use rock to make jewellery.

Quiz

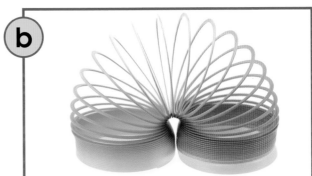

Which of these things are made of rock?

Answer on page 24.

Picture glossary

carve cut into shapes

chalk soft rock. Chalk can be used for drawing.

Index

The **chalk (a)** and **stones (c)** are made of rock.

Notes for parents and teachers
Before reading
Ask children if they have heard the term "material" and what they think it means. Reinforce the concept of materials. Explain that all objects are made from different materials. A material is something that takes up space and can be used to make other things. Ask children to give examples of different materials. These may include metal, wood, and rock.

To get children interested in the topic, ask if they know what rock is. Identify any misconceptions they may have. Ask them to think about whether their ideas might change as the book is read.

After reading
- Check to see if any of the identified misconceptions have changed.
- Show students examples of rock, including chalk, salt, and pebbles.
- Pass the objects round the children. Ask them to describe the properties of each object. What colour is the rock? Is it heavy or light? Big or small? Discuss other words for rock, including stone and pebble.